THE
VW BEETLE
STORY

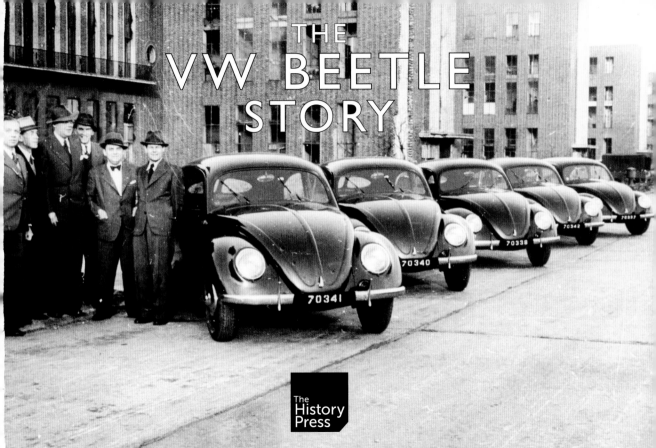

The
History
Press

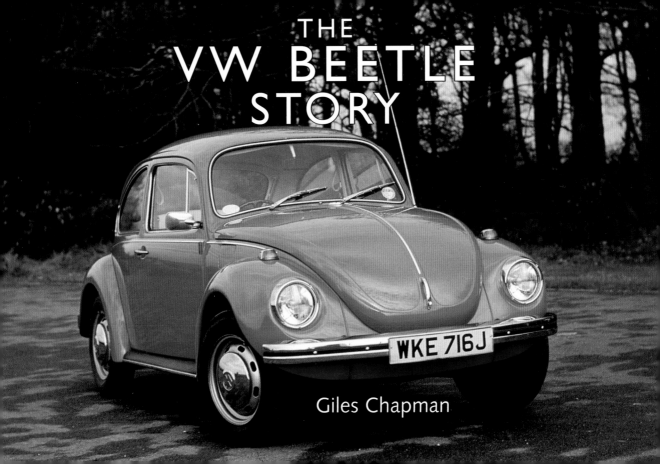

THE
VW BEETLE
STORY

Giles Chapman

Published in the United Kingdom in 2012 by
The History Press
The Mill · Brimscombe Port ·
Stroud · Gloucestershire · GL5 2QG
www.thehistorypress.co.uk

Reprinted 2014, 2019

British Library Cataloguing in Publication Data
A catalogue record for this book is available from the British
Library.

ISBN 978-0-7524-8460-0

Typesetting and origination by The History Press
Printed in China

CONTENTS

This book is about the most successful car the world has ever known. And while, strangely, it isn't the most influential automobile ever, nor the most exciting – and certainly not the fastest – the Volkswagen Beetle still commands respect and adoration everywhere. Okay, the post-modern motoring worlds of India and China never really experienced the car but, everywhere else, people just love the Beetle. And that's an astonishing achievement for a product conceived some eight decades ago.

I got an interesting insight into this a few years back when, while taking a break from writing actual car books, I worked as the 'authenticity guy' with a pal who was creating some car-themed T-shirts incorporating the look of the classic Haynes Manual. The range included various well-known and well-liked vehicles but sales of the Beetle T-shirt out-stripped all others (except the VW Camper one) by a country mile. They couldn't spin the cotton fast enough to make more, and I started to notice them on dads and kids in any high street, shopping centre, airport or major attraction I visited.

A psychologist would probably put that down to the Beetle's rounded contours and friendly visage. For not everyone sporting a Haynes Beetle T-shirt today would realise that the little Volkswagen really is a car you can trust, with its awesome reputation for durability, but perhaps that message is relayed about the wearer in some deeply subconscious way.

Whoa! Enough psycho-babble. Just how successful was the Beetle? Well, over a period from 1939 to 2003, 21,529,464 examples found appreciative new owners.

Some will point out Toyota has sold 37.5m Corollas and Ford in the USA has

shifted 35m F-Series pick-ups, even the Volkswagen Golf has been bought 27.5m times, and ongoing, but the thing about these statistics is that they refer to brand names. Yes, over 35 million cars *called* the Toyota Corolla have been bought, but they've been of several very different designs both aesthetically and mechanically.

While few individual components were actually interchangeable between the earliest and the final Beetles, the cars were fundamentally exactly the same, with almost every facet of the original design robustly intact. Indeed, there is a very massive gap between the Beetle's total sales tally and the next five most successful individual car designs – No. 2, Ford Model T: 15,007,033 between 1908 and 1927; No. 3, VAZ (Lada) 2101–2107/Fiat 124/Seat 124/Tofas/Premier 113E (they're all basically the same car): 14m from 1966 and ongoing; No. 4, Fiat Uno: 8.8m from 1983 and ongoing; and No. 5, Renault 4: 8,135,422 between 1961 and 1993.

Just how did the Beetle manage it? Read on to find out, and also to discover how Volkswagen resurrected a legend to create a characterful new Beetle for the boring lookalike car world of today.

◄ The Volkswagen Beetle, here in its mid-1970s guise, is the best-selling single car design of all time, and likely to stay that way.

Long, long before the very idea of building a motor car accessible to even the least well-off German citizen was hatched, the engineering genius behind it had begun his career in the nascent car industry. Ferdinand Porsche, as a young man, had an appetite for hard work and research to make even today's generation of China's middle-class teenage mathematicians seem indolent and slapdash.

Born on 3 September 1887 in what, today, is the fringe of the Czech Republic where it meets Austria, Ferdinand's parents were hard-working German-speakers, and it was his family duty to help his father in his mechanical engineering workshop. From the very start, he showed an amazing aptitude for the work and, despite a tiring day toiling at his dad's elbow, attended the Imperial Technical School in Reichenberg in the evenings to pack in as much study as

possible. It wasn't long before his talent was spotted by Vienna's Béla Egger Electrical company, and at 18 he moved to the city

◄ *Father of the 'people's car' Dr Ferdinand Porsche, left, with his son and heir Ferdinand 'Ferry' Porsche.*

Did You Know?

The name 'Beetle' was first applied to the car by a journalist writing in the *New York Times* on 3 June 1938; he commented that its contours reminded him of a 'shiny little Beetle'. Yet the car only became a Beetle officially 30 years later.

➤ *This 1900 Lohner-Porsche has electric motors as its front wheels' hubs. One of Porsche's earliest automotive brainwaves.*

to take up a full-time job there in 1893. In view of his subsequent achievements, it's incredible to remember this was the sum total of his purely academic achievement. Everything else came from within him and working 'on the job'.

And in that job, over the next five years, he created and perfected an electric wheel hub motor, moving to carriage-maker Jakob Lohner in 1898 where they were fitted to an early car so that his 'System Lohner-Porsche' could bring it to life. Once that

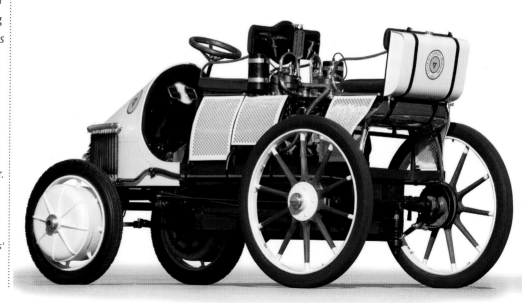

For the powerful
Mercedes-Benz
SSK of the 1920s,
Porsche devised the
first supercharger
seen on a production
sports car.

➤ *This little NSU prototype of 1933 was a true Volkswagen ancestor, in its torsion-bar suspension as well as its shape.*

was up and running smoothly, he next devised the Lohner Mixte, effectively the world's first petrol-electric hybrid car – an idea popularised by Toyota almost 100 years later.

After then enjoying a stellar reputation in the motor industry, Porsche became chief engineer at carmaker Austro-Daimler in 1906. By 1916 he was running the entire firm, but the offer to become technical director at Benz in Germany naturally proved irresistible. Benz and Daimler merged in 1926, and Porsche's subsequent work for the new company included such groundbreakers as the Mercedes-Benz SSK, the first supercharged sports car.

You'd think the technical triumphs and corporate glory would have made Dr Porsche – his honorary title was bestowed in 1917 by Vienna Technical University – a contented individual happy to enjoy the material fruits of his labours. No doubt he was proud of his standing in the business, but the future, as he saw it, didn't contain just the powerful and expensive cars that Austro-Daimler and Mercedes-Benz specialised in. He foresaw the time when the man in the street would fast-track from walking and using buses or trams through bicycles and motorbikes to a small car whose refined technology would make it a part of daily life, rather than some esoteric hobby. The vast majority of small cars in the 1920s were weird contraptions powered by motorbike engines; the stand-out option among them was the Austin Seven, a 'real car in miniature' with four wheels, four seats and four cylinders. But its feebleness and home-spun charm weren't quite in line with Porsche's ideals – he intended to do better.

Not that his colleagues at Mercedes-Benz were enthusiastic. They had come to the correct conclusion that, in general, small cars generated small profits. Keen to nurture his new brainchild, Porsche headed back to Austria for a leading role with local car company Steyr, which was keen to build the kind of car he envisaged. With dreadful timing, the 1929 Wall Street Crash then plunged the world into deep recession; Steyr was in financial trouble and Porsche lost his job.

Now completely undaunted by what life could throw at him, Dr Ferdinand Porsche decided to go it alone. In 1931, in Stuttgart, he established 'Dr. req. h.c. F. Porsche GmbH, Konstruktionen und Beratungen für Motoren und Fahrzeugba'. The company's title implied it would build car engines and bodies; in fact, it was a pure design consultancy, and recruited many of Dr Porsche's most talented former colleagues and contacts. He wasted no time in getting his experiments underway in a series of prototypes built for German manufacturers. First came motorbike firm Zundapp, with a mind to entering the car world, and Porsche devised for it a rear-engined machine with an unusual five-cylinder radial engine; the prototype is said to have driven 6 miles before catastrophic engine failure, and the venture was abandoned. In 1933, Porsche was working for another motorcycle company that would, in time, also become a carmaker: NSU. This time, the prototype used novel torsion-bar suspension, while its power unit was an air-cooled flat-four concealed in its tapering rear end.

The Zundapp and NSU are genuine ancestors of the Beetle, rolling testbeds, no less – the NSU especially. The date when the car itself was fully conceived can actually be pinned to 17 January 1934, a Wednesday, when Dr Porsche submitted his proposal entitled *Exposé concerning the construction of a German people's car* to the German Transport Ministry of the Third Reich. In it, Porsche stated it should be 'an entirely serviceable car of normal dimensions'; that it should be 'a practical means of transportation'; that a 'simple interchange of bodies should make it all-purpose'; and that it should be 'as foolproof as possible, and with all forms of maintenance reduced to a practicable minimum'.

His timing, and his thinking about creating a 'volks wagen' (people's car) via the German Government rather than motor industry enterprise, was spot on. The idea appealed enormously to the Nazi regime, with its nationalistic ideals, even if the reaction from other German carmakers was lukewarm. Porsche's reputation as an innovator with a brilliant tack record also boded well.

Just three months later, a model of the car was exhibited at the Berlin motor show,

It's 1936 and the Type 3 Volks Wagen prototypes hit the road, covering up to 800km of test driving every day.

Did You Know?

Adolf Hitler personally approved the name KdF – standing for Kraft durch Freude and meaning Strength through Joy – for the Volks Wagen (People's Car). Its designer Dr Ferdinand Porsche, and his son Ferry Porsche, were both horrified, apparently.

➤ *This painting from around 1936 captures the scene of VW 30 prototypes taking a breather outside Dr Porsche's country home.*

and on 22 June 1934 the Government gave the project its blessing by instructing Porsche to press ahead with designing the car. His contract stated that he had 10 months to prepare a roadgoing prototype, at a fee of 20,000 Reichsmarks a month. Ever the perfectionist, Porsche was able to prove to his paymasters that more time was needed to get the thing right, and his contract was extended by a year. This was principally because the car would be chock-full of innovative technology to make it a no-brainer in everyday use with the average citizen. Factors that needed time to research and perfect included the horizontally-opposed engine for sustained, all-day driving at continuous speeds on Germany's planned network of *autobahn* motorways, a pressed steel floorpan construction so the car would be strong and rigid – and therefore safe – and torsion-bar independent suspension for a good compromise between comfort and roadholding. 'Foolproof equipment' was Porsche's continual mantra.

In a steady stream of propaganda to stoke public interest – 1 in 49 Germans owned a car, against 1 in 21 Brits – it was announced prototypes would begin testing in the summer of 1935. In fact, the first saloon prototype was presented in July that year and completed in October, but only in February 1936 did an experimental convertible and saloon hit the road. All Beetle aficionados today would recognise the saloon's rounded profile and flat windscreen, although the 'frog-eye' headlights atop the bonnet, and many other details, were different. Fundamentally, a two-stroke twin-cylinder engine was quickly ditched in favour of a four-stroke four.

From 22 October to 22 December 1936, these so-called Type 3 vehicles were

Did You Know?
The first Type 3 prototype cars covered 850,000 miles in development testing, often driven round the clock by a team of 200 SS soldiers who thrashed them ruthlessly. By comparison, a prototype Ford of the mid-1930s would typically cover 20,000 test miles.

subjected to a mammoth test programme, with Porsche's test drivers covering up to 800km a day in continuous driving, fastidiously recording their performance findings in fat ledgers. In daylight hours, Type 3s chugged along country roads in the Black Forest, or pounded the *autobahn* between Stuttgart and Bad Nauheim, and during the night running repairs and workshop adjustments would be made. Each car covered 50,000km (30,000 miles) as gremlins were ironed out – these kinds of tests are normal now but were unheard of in the mid-1930s. Meanwhile, with German car manufacturers still reluctant to have the 'volks wagen' rolling off their own production lines, Ferdinand Porsche went to the USA to take notes on mass-production techniques in factories owned by Detroit giants such as Ford and General Motors. His findings would help shape plans for a plant, financed by the German Government, with the audacious target of making 1m cars annually.

The People's Car venture was slowly gathering its own, important momentum.

The painstaking thoroughness of the Type 30 test programme, and the satisfactory results, led to the next stage of the project: building the cars. A much-modified design emerged in 1937, the VW 30. You only need the briefest of looks at it to see it was very close to the final form the Beetle would take. The significance of its title was the scheme to assemble 30 identical examples, using a real-life production line provided by Mercedes-Benz and bodywork from the Reutter coachworks. This was the test to see how efficiently the cars could be bolted together and then, as each one was completed, it joined a new testing programme that saw the VW 30s collectively cover 2.4km.

In May 1937, the German Government set up a company in Berlin called GEZUVOR, which by September 1938 had been rechristened with the slightly catchier Volkswagenwerk GmbH. With 50m Reichmarks of finance at its disposal, and 30m already lavished on creating the car itself, the organisation was tasked with building the factory and making the cars. This was made much easier than it might have been in, say, the UK because the Third Reich simply chose a location – the village of Fallersleben, 50 miles east of Hanover – that was convenient for transport links, and then ordered the German Labour Front to provide the manpower to build it. Oh, yes, and an entire adjoining town (with its own hospital) to house the factory workers. It all seems so easy when you rule with an iron fist. . . .

The cornerstone for the plant was laid on 26 May 1938, and construction started immediately. As the former farmland was torn up, the site was known as 'KdF-Stadt'. The acronym stood for Kraft durch Freude,

Did You Know?
In 1938 the Porsche Apprentice School built five 1:12.5 scale models of the KdF-Wagen as gifts. One of them went to Hitler, another to Porsche and another to electrical tycoon Dr Robert Bosch. Bosch's model was sold for £42,000 at auction in the 1990s.

meaning Strength through Joy, so the place was The Town of The Strength Through Joy Car – sinister-sounding, Orwellian stuff indeed.

In fact, Kraft durche Freude was the name of the Third Reich's 'Ministry of Leisure', a department dedicated to making formerly middle-class pursuits like holidays and travel available, and affordable, for every citizen. Nazi top brass had decided KdF would be in charge of a groundbreaking hire purchase scheme allowing even relatively poor people to buy a Volkswagen. It would be a coupons-based savings plan through which Germans could order and pay for a KdF car in three variants (saloon with or without sunroof, and a convertible), costing 990 Reichsmarks, in weekly bites of just 5 Reichsmarks. The factory's gigantic manufacturing capacity indicated the grandeur of the roll-out of both car and purchasing scheme; it was expected to churn out 500,000 cars a year in its first stage, eventually rising to 1m. And by the end of 1938, just under 170,000 savings accounts had been opened by people keen to get their hands on one of the cars. For the production-ready version,

trumpeted as the Type 38, was unveiled in April 1938 gaining, unsurprisingly, blanket coverage and approval in the daily papers; the curvaceous shape with headlights faired into the front mudguards was already a national icon.

◄ By 1938, the production-ready Volkswagen was unveiled, and a profile that became world-famous was ready for its public.

▲ *The Nazis' KdF scheme allowed for three versions of the Volkswagen – a saloon, a sunroof-saloon and a cabriolet, seen here in 1938 prototype form.*

➤ *In 1938, a fleet of KdFs toured Germany (here, Berlin) to promote the car and the Government-backed savings scheme for citizens to buy one.*

◀◀ *This facility in Brunswick was opened in 1938 to train Volkswagen engineers; the 'VW' on the gatehouse is one of the earliest known uses of the iconic logo.*

◀ *Dr Porsche with a late KdF prototype; he was said to be dismayed at how his big idea was exploited for political ends.*

Versuchswagen

IIIA - 43011

Examples of the car toured the nation's towns and cities in 1939, complete with customer-ready running boards and bumpers. Halfway through the year, the first machinery began to be installed in the plant, much of it sourced from the USA, at the same time as an academy facility was opened in Brunswick to train apprentices to become plant engineers. But it was at this point, of course, world events rather overtook the German people's car venture. War was declared in September 1939 and the immediate order was given to cease construction. For those hoping to get behind the wheel of a brand new car for the very first time, the prospect seemed as remote as it ever had.

When the Second World War ended, with Germany bowed and beaten, the dust settled on the rubble of the Volkswagenwerk plant. Two-thirds of it lay in bombed-out ruins, with the damage estimated to have cost 156m Reichsmarks. Allied bombers had done everything they could to flatten it entirely because almost immediately after war had been declared, the newly built factory had been turned over to armaments manufacture – including various types of four-wheel drive Kubelwagen (meaning 'bucket car') field cars exclusively for the German Army. By 1945, 52,000 of them had been built, along with another 14,000 amphibious vehicles called Schwimmwagens, so the place was a key part of the Nazis' war apparatus. Dwarfed by these were the 630 Volkswagen cars also produced from 15 August 1940 onwards.

However, despite the pounding inflicted on the place, with 73 lives lost and 160 of the 9,000 workers injured, the plant was never quite put totally out of action. Valuable machinery was transferred to other sites so it wouldn't be obliterated

▼ *The Volkswagen plant at Wolfsburg, seen from the air; to this day, it remains the biggest car factory on earth.*

Did You Know?

Some 336,000 savers never did get their cars through the Nazis' KdF hire-purchase scheme, and their outstanding legal claims for compensation weren't settled until 1960.

➤ *The KdF plant at Wolfsburg built these Kubelwagens (literally: bucket cars) for the German Army during the WW2. In peace-time, they made cheap runabouts.*

yet assembly continued in the factory itself throughout the war.

In 1943 the British Army managed to seize a military Volkswagen Type 82 Kubelwagen, and asked British carmaker the Rootes Group to assess its merits. The damning verdict was that it was 'not an example of first-rate modern design'. Nonetheless,

a British secret intelligence team remained convinced of the significance of the Volkswagen and the giant Fallersleben factory. 'The Volkswagen is the most advanced and the most interesting for quantity production,' it said in its German car review. It could, they continued, offer 'a possible solution to the cheap utility vehicle that would be acceptable [in the UK] and in the overseas market.'

The first task that befell the British Military Government, the Allied force in charge of the area, was to sweep away all the KdF nonsense. This it did at a meeting of the town council on 25 May 1945 when the place (population: 17,000) was renamed Wolfsburg, after a local castle, and the plant was temporarily renamed the Wolfsburg Motor Works.

Colonel Charles Radclyffe – a member of the Control Commission for Germany and the man responsible for the British

Army's motor vehicles in the occupied zone – had already picked over the remains, and had set about using the few undamaged buildings and machines to patch up damaged army trucks and scout cars. Soon 500 men were hard at work, and a young British Army officer named Major Ivan Hirst was then transferred to Wolfsburg from a tank repair depot in Brussels to determine what could be salvaged from it. Hirst later said, 'Nobody gave me a real brief – I was just told to go there and do something. I'd first read about the car in 1939 but didn't give it much thought, really.'

Hirst had to decide in August 1945 whether the Volkswagen Kubelwagen or the saloon would be the best choice to put back into production to put local services like the post office and doctors on wheels. One Colonel Michael McEvoy had ridden in the pre-war saloon prototype, and was enthusiastic about it. 'He understood [its] potential as desperately needed transport for the occupying forces,' Hirst recalled. 'The British had nothing smaller than a dirty great "light" truck, and the rail network had all but been bombed out of existence.' So the saloon it was.

The crucial production machinery, mothballed around Germany, was quickly rounded up, and manufacture began, thoroughly and calmly organised and overseen by the pipe-smoking Hirst. The factory's toilets were blocked, two-thirds of its roof and most of its windows were missing, and scarce components had to be sourced from, for instance, camera manufacturers to complete the first cars, so it was some achievement that, by the end of 1945, 1,785 cars had been completed. These cars, with raised suspension, were delivered to the Army and the German Post Office. Proper series production of the definitive, final-specification Beetle began in December

The banner says it all, but at the wheel is Ivan Hirst, the placid British Army major responsible for resurrecting the whole Volkswagen project.

1945, with 55 examples completed that month. Hirst set a production target of 1,000 cars for March 1946 and, to everyone's surprise, it was met. The RAF put in an order for 50 blue cars, and 100 light grey ones went to the French military.

Under Hirst's command, quality improved amazingly fast, as the rebuilding process carried on all around the production lines. His ingenuity was of huge benefit; he once bartered a car for a truckload of coal, worked out a way of welding the large roof panel from two small pieces of steel, and had no problem with asking other factories to help out. 'They were, after all, desperate for work,' he remembered. When nothing better was available, Hirst secured supplies of fish glue to keep assembly rolling.

Soldiers of the British occupying forces could buy a Volkswagen for a concessionary £100 and take it home, but very few chose to. One that did find its way to Britain was bought by John Colborne-Baber, owner of Colborne Garages in Ripley, Surrey, who registered it as JLT 420. After 10 days of driving it, he became so convinced it would be a winner in his showroom that he drove it back to Wolfsburg to obtain an import agreement. A short time later he sold the first few to UK-based customers, mainly Kent-based US Air Force personnel already familiar with them. Observers must have thought him a maverick weirdo, because the attitude of the British motor industry towards Wolfsburg and its products was loftily dismissive. No-one wanted to take it on as a spoil of war.

A commission headed by carmaking grandee Lord Rootes concluded: 'The vehicle does not meet the fundamental technical requirements of a motor car. . . . As regards performance and design, it is quite unattractive to the average motor car buyer. It is too ugly and too noisy. To build the car commercially would be a completely uneconomic enterprise.' Rootes couldn't resist bellowing at Major Ivan Hirst, 'If you think you're going to build cars here, young man, you're a bloody fool.' By the end of 1946, annual production under the bespectacled major had soared to 10,000, restricted only by shortages of raw materials; 'My personal view is that the Beetle should have needled the British car industry into doing better,' the elderly Hirst told *Top Gear* magazine in 1999.

The production Volkswagen itself had finally emerged into the post-war period pretty much in the form in which it was signed off in 1938.

It was a small four-seater saloon that, thanks to its air-cooled engine, would not ice up in winter or overheat in summer. The four-cylinder engine of 1131cc (up from the previous 985cc) was positioned horizontally at the back, and produced 25bhp of power at 3,300rpm. This gave it a top speed of just 65mph (105km/h). To keep the engine ventilated, a belt-driven radial flow fan in a steel housing was installed above the engine on an extended alternator shaft, and the power unit was tipped forwards slightly to accommodate the fan under the car's sloping tail. The single dry-plate clutch, four-speed gearbox and final drive were contained in one housing, and the exhaust was positioned transversely behind the engine initially with one tailpipe but later two.

Some rear-engined cars later developed a scary reputation for instability, but the gutlessness and light weight of the early Volkswagen – the whole car weighed just 720kg – did make it pretty fool-proof, as Dr Porsche had intended. The torsion-bar suspension was independent all round, with friction dampers. The fuel tank under the 'bonnet' could hold 41 litres, and there was a reserve tank of 5 litres, which was perfectly adequate as the car could manage

▼ *Here it is, the basic 'Volkswagen Limousine' (saloon) that was, in the late 1940s, the very first version to go on widespread public sale.*

a thrifty average fuel economy of 7.5 litres per 100km. But there wasn't much space for luggage under the bonnet that Porsche had carefully shaped to be aerodynamic. Inside, it was austere but functional, in the true style of the 1930s Bauhaus design movement, with rotary control knobs and an open glove compartment either side of the steering wheel.

Sales of the Volkswagen to the public were slow to start, as most of the first 20,000 cars were ordered by and supplied to the Allied occupying forces for their duties in getting German reconstruction underway. British Army drivers, therefore, were the ones to endure early teething problems, which included flaking paint and instant rust spots, windscreens and headlights that cracked easily, and doors and bonnets that wouldn't shut properly. As the car's actual design was more than sound, quick-witted managers put a quality regime in place, focused upon the quality of components *before* the cars were actually assembled. So rapidly did the Volkswagen improve in build quality that Pon Brothers in the Netherlands gladly opened up the first export market, taking an initial 56 cars in August 1947 and providing valuable feedback. Indeed, it was the Pons who persuaded Volkswagen to introduce the Transporter van in 1950.

A chaotic German economy, however, where cigarettes were a more stable currency than the Reichsmark and price controls had been in force since 1936, meant home sales were minimal until 1948, with major currency reforms in June that year. The painful process of converting the old Reichsmarks to the new Deutschmarks meant the value of most people's savings were wiped out – it was a 1 for 10 rate up to 600 Marks, a 1 for 1 thereafter – but from hereon in Volkswagen could trade properly, and obtain supplies through stable transactions rather than the barter system that had often been used so far. German sales of the car, at 5,300DM, continued to be tiny, but production gathered pace. The 25,000th car was built in May 1948, and from then until November monthly output rose from 1,185 to 2,306 as raw materials arrived in an orderly fashion. The 50,000th car was built in May 1949. The 'normalisation' continued with a gradual return of the plant to German control. Radclyffe and Hirst appointed exceptionally talented young ex-Opel manager Heinrich Nordhoff as the man to lead Volkswagen in peacetime, who took the post only if his decisions could not be overruled by the British authorities. He had the sort of attitude that impressed British military chiefs; 'Service is not just a question of salesmen in white coats,' he said in 1950. 'It is a question of inner attitude.'

Consequently, in September 1949, Ivan Hirst departed Wolfsburg for good, his job done.

Apart from cars bought by German businesses, some 15 per cent of Volkswagens were bound for export, with batches of cars dispatched to Belgium, Denmark, Luxembourg, Norway, Sweden and Switzerland. On 8 January 1949, a pair was sent to the USA by the enterprising Pon Brothers as a toe-in-the-water exercise to gauge reaction.

▲ An important day at Wolfsburg in 1947 as the Dutch Pon brothers (on right, Ben Pon second in) accept the first consignment of export Volkswagens.

There was a stark contrast between the attitudes of car manufacturers from victorious Britain and the beaten Germans in the post-war export battle. The Brits sent what they built and were affronted when the complaints came back that their cars were lacking – such as the early Morris Minor, which was too feeble to tackle the hills of San Francisco, or the Standard Vanguard, whose poor door seals meant the cabin filled up with dust. Volkswagen, already blessed with a rugged basic design, reacted to feedback by launching, on 1 June 1949, the 'Export' model. Here was the start of the Volkswagen as the world would soon come to know it.

➤ *Chrome bumpers and hubcaps, plus a range of cheerful colours, distinguished the new Export version of the Volkswagen in 1949.*

Outwardly, the car benefited from a wide range of bright paint colours such as red, pastel green and mid-brown (instead of just black or grey), chrome trim, bumpers and domed hubcaps with a red VW logo, and a vastly improved and more

◀ The earliest Volkswagens had a pretty functional dashboard and two very useful open gloveboxes at either end.

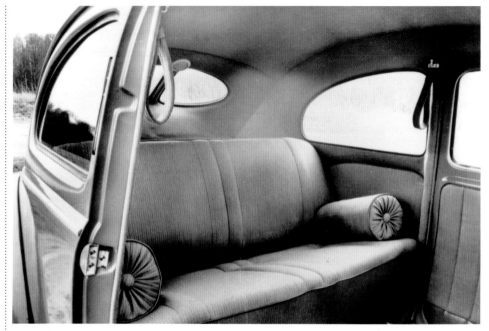

➤ *The quite inviting rear seats of the 1949 Export; behind the seat back is a deep if not particularly convenient storage compartment.*

Did You Know?

The chrome-laden Export model, introduced in 1949, was also offered on the German home market. By 1957, it was outselling the basic car in Germany by 20 to 1.

comfortable interior. But unseen worthwhile improvements included hydraulic brakes and a damped steering system to make driving the car less jarring.

On the very same day, Volkswagen also lifted the lid on two types of convertible, both with bodywork from outside coachbuilders. One, the Hebmüller

Type 14a, was a two-seater with a long, elegant, sloping tail and a hood that was completely concealed when folded. Volkswagen ordered 675 of these beauties but a catastrophic fire at the Hebmüller plant and the company's subsequent closure ensured that only a little over 700 were ever made. They are extremely rare and collectable today.

The other open Volkswagen was Karmann's four-seater Type 15 cabriolet, with its high-quality, fully lined hood stacked up at the back when folded as on a pram. Based on the Export model, it was destined, by contrast to the Hebmüller, for an extraordinarily long and successful production run, and it was loved by celebrity drivers in the 1950s like Brigitte Bardot, Alain Delon, Pierre Cardin and Yves Saint Laurent.

In 1950, the Volkswagen went properly global; with its Export model coming on stream, Volkswagen made its first official shipment of 328 cars to the USA – a market where the car would soon enjoy extraordinary success pitted against the Detroit establishment. And in November, assembly of cars sent in completely knocked-down (CKD) kit form would begin in Brazil, prising open another territory for the car and the company; a similar arrangement soon followed in South Africa.

Yet the Volkswagen's first international impact was much closer to home as far as British customers were concerned. The very first CKD assembly operation was in Dublin, beginning in the second half of 1950. The search to find someone willing to assemble it in Britain had been fruitless, so VW instead turned to Irish entrepreneur Denis Connolly, and the success of his venture made him a millionaire within two years, and eventually saw 83,000 Volkswagens produced there up to 1968.

➤ *Only a few hundred of these cute Hebmüller roadsters were made before a disastrous fire destroyed the production line.*

Did You Know?
Unusually, the original 'Beetle' saloon and convertible (with its roof up) were equally as aerodynamic, sharing a drag co-efficient figure of 0.49.

◄ *The Hebmüller was particularly neat from the rear – its rarity means the few survivors are highly prized today.*

43

➤ *The cabriolet convertible, with handsome bodywork built by Karmann of Osnabrück, was another debutante of 1949.*

Improvements to the car came thick and fast. In 1950, an optional fabric sunroof, followed in 1951 by telescopic shock absorbers replacing lever-arm dampers and the appearance of the Wolfsburg coat of arms emblem on the Export model, and in 1952 by synchromesh on second to fourth gears and proper rear brake lights – before, there had been just one, which doubled as the number plate light! Swivelling front quarter lights were also welcomed by drivers, as was a redesigned dashboard with a single glove compartment.

Volkswagen sales officially began in the UK in 1952 with the establishment of Volkswagen Motors in London's St John's Wood. A year later, with a handful of cars sold, James Graydon joined the company

FACTS & DATA: VOLKSWAGEN 'EXPORT'

Announced: 1949
Engine capacity: 1131cc
Engine bore/stroke: 75/64mm
Engine power output: 25bhp @ 3400rpm
Fuel system: single-carburettor
Bodystyle: two-door, four-seater saloon or convertible
Wheelbase: 2400mm
Length: 4070mm
Width: 1540mm
Height: 1500mm
Top speed: 65mph
Acceleration, 0-60mph: 28.9sec
Fuel consumption, average: 35mpg
Price when new: £689 (in 1954)

with a brief to turn it into the largest importer of foreign cars in Britain. With solid motor industry experience, he succeeded in building up sales of Volkswagens in those early days.

When *The Autocar* first road-tested an Export saloon, the car wasn't even on official sale in the UK, although its 5,150DM price then equated to £439 without Purchase Tax. In the starchy language of the times, the magazine positively raved about the car, saying 'it's easy for any driver to obtain the best performance from the car,' and 'the synchromesh cannot be beaten, either on slow changes or on snap full-throttle changes; the gears always engage silently and easily.' It rated the handling as 'really very good' and the suspension 'exceptionally good for a small car', while brakes, driving position, heating and standards of finish all gained unreserved approval. The conclusion was straight:

'A roadworthy, robust small car. . . . It gives a good performance without effort.'

The first significant style change for the Volkswagen Type 1 (the Transporter van and kombi series was the Type 2) arrived in 1953, to the dismay of those who love the pure design ethos of the original.

▼ *On the left, James Graydon, the businessman who built Volkswagen's fortunes in Britain; on the right, Leonard Wagstaff winning a new Volkswagen 1500 in 1964 after his existing car had won a competition to find this country's best-kept 1953 VW.*

▲ More Volkswagens setting off on their export journey to new owners, in this case a pair travelling by train through Switzerland.

➤ A sliding/folding fabric sunroof was one of the most popular early options on the 'split-window' Volkswagen.

▲ What Ferdinand did next: Dr Porsche helped his son Ferry to create the first Porsche sports cars, based on the Volkswagen. Here they are together with an early example in 1948.

Did You Know?
In 1951, Volkswagen carried out feasibility tests with a diesel-engined car. Lack of power, too much noise, and the fact the car had to be warmed up while stationary before moving off, meant the project was soon ditched.

From March, all new cars now came with a one-piece oval rear screen, in place of the pretzel-shaped split-screen that had been forced on Dr Porsche by 1930s glass technology and cost restrictions. The new one-piece rear screen shared the contours of the Volkswagen's tail but was barely more use for actually seeing out of!

Here, fully-finished bodies are lowered to marry up with their driveline components of engines and gearboxes.

▶▶ Shiny new Volkswagens rolling off the end of the Wolfsburg production line in about 1954.

On 8 August 1955, Volkswagen built its millionth vehicle, this oval-window saloon, and painted it a gleaming gold to celebrate.

With manufacturing quality and comfort taken care of, Volkswagen's engineers next looked at the car's modest power output and decided to give it a boost. The result was the new 1200 model in 1954, with an enlarged 1192cc engine producing 30bhp, which meant a top speed increase to 70mph.

This gutsier VW was a significant contributor to the increasing sales that led to the major milestone of 1955: the one millionth example produced. The big day itself was 8 August. The car carried the flag for the unfolding German 'economic miracle' as the country got back to productive work after the Second World War, and by now accounted for 50 per cent of all car production there. Wolfsburg was turning out 1,000 cars a day, of which over a third set sail for existing export markets, including new assembly plants in Belgium, Australia, New Zealand and, most importantly of all, Mexico. There was huge

celebration at all Volkswagen outposts, not least of which was Volkswagen of America Inc, the wholly-owned US importer which opened for business that year and immediately became the biggest US car importer as it pole-vaulted over the previous leader: our very own Austin. In 1956, the new company sold an impressive 46,000 cars. The instant success could be attributed to both the innate soundness of the car and the good customer service provided by the dealers – many of them German émigrés – at a time when many domestic manufacturers had an embedded, take-it-or-leave-it arrogance.

After four more years of terrible rearward vision, Volkswagen replaced the tiny oval window in its saloons with a large rectangular one at the end of 1957, with double the surface area. Although there would be many minor tweaks to the look of the car in the coming years, this would

Did You Know?
When the split rear window was replaced by a one-piece oval screen, Volkswagen offered a kit to convert existing earlier cars to the newer rear window style. This meant, of course, that some restorers later had to convert them back to the more desirable early look loved by collectors!

be the last major external change for 13 years. The car had become frozen in time but, with one being made every minute – boosted by yet another new assembly plant in the Philippines – its worldwide success continued unabated, and by 1962 the five millionth example had been sold.

The year 1959 saw two really worthwhile improvements to the cars. First there was an uprated engine now giving 34bhp, and second was a gearbox that, finally, had synchromesh on first gear so the car became simpler to drive for the newcomer. The size of the luggage compartment also went up by 65 per cent, push-button door handles were neater and more ergonomic, and indicator lights replaced semaphore arms.

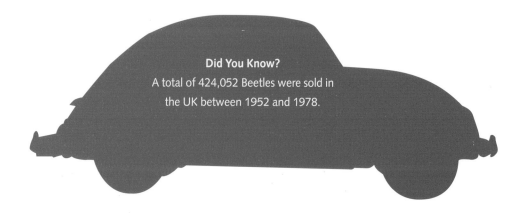

Did You Know?
A total of 424,052 Beetles were sold in
the UK between 1952 and 1978.

Careful, evolutionary changes made to Volkswagens contrasted markedly with the so-called 'planned obsolescence' strategy used by American and, to a lesser extent, British carmakers; every year, a cosmetically adjusted new model would render last year's out of date. And there was a similar difference in advertising. After New York ad agency Doyle Dane Bernbach won the Volkswagen account in 1959 and launched the 'Think small' campaign, a revolution in talking to potential customers was underway. Out went distorted illustrations and patronising sales hype and in came a witty, pared-back and honest approach. As the introduction to the book *Remember those great Volkswagen ads?* says: 'The copy talked to the reader as though he were an intelligent friend, not some distant moron, and was self-deprecating rather than self-congratulatory.'

Der grosse Tag...
endlich VW-Besitzer

Did You Know?
A TV commercial for the VW Beetle once asked how the man who drives a snowplough gets to work. 'This one drives a Volkswagen. Mystery solved.'

◄ *German Volkswagen advertising in the 1950s celebrated nothing more complicated than the arrival of a new car in the family, often for the very first time.*

The all-time classic is the 'Lemon' ad, where Volkswagen admits its cars sometimes have small faults (which are picked up by

▲ *This is a British-market Volkswagen 1200 in 1960 with a more practical, rectangular rear window, an uprated 34bhp engine, and – finally – synchromesh on first gear.*

quality inspectors), but there were dozens of others, such as the photo of a typical suburban house with a Volkswagen parked outside and the line 'What year car do the Jones drive?' (you can't tell); and a picture of a Volkswagen being towed by a breakdown truck with the caption: 'A rare photo.' Other ads picked up on the car's real-life attributes, such as its high resale value with the line 'Before buying a car you should think about how you're going to get rid of it.' Or the fact that repairs, and hence running costs, were cheap '. . . Because it needs so few.'

DDB brought its groundbreaking style to the UK too, epitomised by an ad featuring a prominent picture of rubber-faced, goggle-eyed comic Marty Feldman with the tagline: 'If he can make it, so can Volkswagen'; and 'It comes in its own garage' – a soundly painted VW parked outside a Victorian London house.

Typical of the self-deprecating style of DDB's highly effective campaign for Volkswagen was the iconic 'Lemon' ad.

Lemon.

This Volkswagen missed the boat.

The chrome strip on the glove compartment is blemished and must be replaced. Chances are you wouldn't have noticed it; Inspector Kurt Kroner did.

There are 3,389 men at our Wolfsburg factory with only one job: to inspect Volkswagens at each stage of production. (3000 Volkswagens are produced daily; there are more inspectors than cars.)

Every shock absorber is tested (spot checking won't do), every windshield is scanned. VWs have been rejected for surface scratches barely visible to the eye.

Final inspection is really something! VW inspectors run each car off the line onto the Funktionsprüfstand (car test stand), tote up 189 check points, gun ahead to the automatic brake stand, and say "no" to one VW out of fifty.

This preoccupation with detail means the VW lasts longer and requires less maintenance, by and large, than other cars. (It also

means a used VW depreciates less than any other car.)

We pluck the lemons; you get the plums.

55

▲ *In 1960s California, ingenious enthusiasts cut away the bodywork, shedding weight and opening up the space for big wheels and tyres, to create the 'Baja Bug' desert racing fun car.*

For many ordinary Germans of the early 1960s, the Beetle represented not only the first opportunity to own a brand new car but also an instant getaway, as thousands set off over the Alps for their first taste of sunshine holidays in Italy, and the first chance to bag a sunlounger with a towel before the Brits had even dreamed of package holidays (it being a rather long and horrible drive from Birmingham to the Med by Standard Ten). Taking a snapshot of the Volkswagen and the smiling family at the Brenner Pass on the Italian border became a part of this national holiday ritual.

Elsewhere, the Beetle was turned into a dragster, a dune buggy and a desert racer

– the shortened, big-wheeled Baja Bug – in the USA, while in Austria a *Guinness Book of Records* entry was achieved when 57 people squeezed into one Volkswagen in a world-beating example of 'Beetle Cramming'.

◄ *Another imaginative, US-invented take on the Beetle was the beach buggy, epitomised by the classic Meyers Manx seen here (picture courtesy James Hale, whose lovely book* The Dune Buggy Phenomenon *tells the whole story).*

One of the car's genuine quirks was ironed out in 1962, when the Export version finally gained a petrol gauge (the rarely ordered standard saloon sticking with its basic, three-position fuel reserve tap). But the juice still had to go through a cap that was under the bonnet until 1967, when the most expensive models finally received an external filler flap just above the front mudguard.

Indeed, over the following few years the cars would blossom into something of a range in an ongoing search for more power in a time of faster roads and longer commutes. Starting in 1965, the standard car now came with the 34bhp engine and the Export version became the 1300, with a 40bhp 1285cc engine which allowed it to reach 75mph. The smaller engine became confined to an austere Economy model from 1967 (Germany was suffering its first post-war recession), the basic Standard models now gaining a 34bhp version of the 1300 engine, while a new 1493cc 1500 version – sharing its power unit with the Transporter vans and campers – was able to manage a raucous 79mph with lots of useful extra poke through the gears. With

FACTS & DATA: VOLKSWAGEN 1300

Announced: 1965
Engine capacity: 1285cc
Engine bore/stroke: 77/69mm
Engine power output: 40bhp @ 3400rpm
Fuel system: single-carburettor
Bodystyle: two-door, four-seater saloon or convertible
Wheelbase: 2400mm
Length: 4030mm
Width: 1550mm
Height: 1500mm
Top speed: 80mph
Acceleration, 0-60mph: 25.4sec
Fuel consumption, average: 34mpg
Price when new: £649 (in 1966)

Did You Know?
After Volkswagen acquired Audi in 1965, Beetle demand was so strong that Audi's Ingolstadt plant was commandeered for temporary extra capacity, turning out 347,869 Beetles up to 1969.

◄ *Automatic Stickshift was American for VW's semi-automatic, clutch-less transmission option, new for '69.*

additional urge, front disc brakes were a desirable standard fitment on this one. Apart from their badges, the easy way to tell a 1300 from a 1500 was by their steering wheels – two-spoke in the 1300 and three-spoke in its brawnier brother. Greater occupant safety was addressed with a collapsible steering column and three-point seatbelts, and a notable first was the availability of a clutch-less semi-automatic Saxomat transmission on the 1500. However, purists were dismayed at the new heavier bumpers also ushered in during 1967, moaning that they looked like railway tracks.

It is amazing today to consider that, until some point between 1967 and '69, Dr Porsche's Volkswagen had officially been called all sorts of things by Wolfsburg, but never the Beetle. It's true. The car was first compared to the curve-backed insect by a journalist in the 1930s, and then John Colborne-Baber's son had to endure jeers of 'beetle!' from school friends whenever his father turned up to collect him in one of the first examples seen in Britain. 'Bug', the American vernacular for anything creepy-crawly and beetle-like, had long been an unofficial nickname in the USA, but only now did Wolfsburg management gradually adopt the Beetle name for its products, by 1969 using it widely on brochures and advertising.

They did this just in time to best capitalise on two rather different Volkswagen-related events in the media.

The Love Bug was the last live-action film actually approved by Walt Disney before he died. The story of a car called Herbie with a mind of its own and No. 53 racing number on his doors was an enormous box office hit, and is required family viewing to this day. The 1963 pearl white, VW sunroof sedan got the part after production staff found it irresistible from a pool of potential star cars parked prospectively outside the studio.

And then, in 1969, popular beat combo The Beatles released their final studio album, *Abbey Road*. As part of one of the most

◄◄ *Herbie, a Volkswagen with a mind of its own, took the starring role in the 1968 Disney movie* The Love Bug.

◄ *Hollywood's special effects guys had a field day with* The Love Bug, *to the delight of children everywhere ever since.*

Did You Know?
The only surviving
example of Herbie
from the 1968 film
The Love Bug with
studio-fitted gadgets
like self-opening doors
and oil-squirters is
owned by the human
star of the movie,
Dean Jones.

➤ *A 1975 Beetle in that defiant mid-1970s colour choice: bright orange.*

◄ Beetle hardware, from engines to the entire chassis, put life into many other cars of 1969: the 181 (top left) and Karmann-Ghia (centre) were official derivatives, while racing cars and beach buggies were separate cottage industries.

iconic record sleeves ever, with the Fab Four walking across a zebra crossing in London NW8, there is a Volkswagen Beetle parked by the roadside. The humble white saloon – which belonged to someone happening to live in the block of flats opposite the

This Beetle-based beach buggy is an Apal C, hailing from Belgium, and there were many others to choose from including Britain's popular GP.

The 1969 Volkswagen 181, with Beetle underpinnings, was a factory-built fun car evoking the war-time Kubelwagen; in the USA, it was sold as The Thing.

famous recording studio – along with its nondescript registration number of LMW 281F, accidentally became one of the planet's most famous motor cars.

The Volkswagen Beetle had finally arrived, 35 years after the car itself had been created. And for a car that had sold more than 10 million copies up to this

point, it was remarkable that it could enjoy a place in the emerging global counterculture. A Beetle was sensible enough for a headmaster but classless and cool enough for any hippie to plaster with floral imagery and hide his stash of grass behind the rear seats in.

The cars were realigned by 1970. A 1584cc, 40bhp engine option was added to the range, which could propel a standard

➤ *Volkswagens, owing to their lack of outright speed, were rarely rally winners, but they generally completed the course, providing entertainment for spectators and drivers alike.*

Beetle past 80mph for the first time ever. But the 1302/1302S 'Super Beetle' series was a new parallel range offering engine options of 1285cc and 1584cc, giving 44 and 55bhp of power respectively in a chassis that now boasted a fully revised suspension system with MacPherson struts and an anti-roll bar at the front allied to a semi-elliptic

▲ Hard to believe Volkswagen managed to liberate 85 per cent more luggage space under the Super Beetle's bonnet while keeping its hallowed profile largely intact.

double-jointed set-up at the back. The S featured front disc brakes and Bosch fuel-injection for the US and Japanese markets. The ride and handling were improved to match the extra power, and the turning circle was decreased. From the windscreen forward, the bodywork retained the usual profile but in fact was all-new and 30cm longer, with a bulkier bonnet for 85 per cent more luggage capacity.

The fact that the 14 millionth Beetle was a car destined for a British customer in

1971 was one of numerous statistical gems in the car's venerable career. Another was that production reached its annual peak in 1971, at 1,292,000. The 15,007,034th, though, really was a groundbreaker. On 17 February 1972, this very car saw the Volkswagen Beetle finally nose ahead of the Ford Model T to become the best-selling single car of all time.

A 1973 replacement for the 1302 was the 1303, now with 44bhp in standard form and also in a fuel-injected 1303S version that was virtually a Lamborghini, relatively speaking, with 50bhp on tap. The main event externally was a prominent, bulging wraparound windscreen that allowed a safer, padded dashboard to be installed. The company also started issuing limited edition Beetles, such as the Jeans Beetle with its natty denim seats.

Yet, despite all this, and continuing massive sales, Volkswagen's management was uncomfortably aware that its business was quirky and eccentric compared to competitors.

◀ For many, the Beetle was simply a working tool, such as this Super Beetle, one of thousands used as German police patrol cars.

➤ By 1971, when this Beetle 1300 was brand new, curved vents were added behind the rear side windows to help through-flow ventilation.

➤➤ The Beetle saw its global annual sales peak in 1971, when this was sold in the UK, at 1,292,000.

➤ The Jeans Beetle was a famous 1974 limited edition loved for its matt-black trim and, of course, its real denim-covered seats.

The car industry's new-found concern with safety as the 1970s dawned saw these crash test dummies help to improve occupant protection in Beetles and other Volkswagens.

Its prosperity depended on the continuing attraction of its cars with air-cooled, flat-four engines at the back. In a VW context, this was an entirely logical and, of course, well-proven configuration, but the momentum at most rival companies – even Fiat, although not some timewarp carmakers behind the Communist 'Iron Curtain' – had shifted to the opposite end of the car.

➤ This 1971 limited edition 1300 Super Vee marked VW's 1971–7 support of Formula Super Vee racing. Extra goodies included Sprintstar sports wheels, overriders, Hella halogen driving lamps, and go-slightly-faster stripes!

➤➤ A jokey limited edition called the GT Beetle arrived in Britain in 1973, offering a 1600 engine and sports wheels for just £19 over a standard 1300. Helmet not included.

FACTS & DATA: VOLKSWAGEN BEETLE 1303S

Announced: 1973
Engine capacity: 1584cc
Engine bore/stroke: 85.5/69mm
Engine power output: 50bhp @ 4000rpm
Fuel system: single-carburettor
Bodystyle: two-door, four-seater saloon or convertible
Wheelbase: 2440mm
Length: 4090mm
Width: 1570mm
Height: 1470mm
Top speed: 82mph
Acceleration, 0-60mph: 17.1sec
Fuel consumption, average: 27mpg
Price when new: £1090 (in 1973)

➤ *The Beetle nudged the Ford Model T off the top spot, held since 1927. Beetle and Model T are still respectively the No. 1 and No. 2 all-time top sellers.*

Pioneered by Britain's Mini, compact cars with a power unit mounted transversely at the front, driving the front wheels, quickly made this the optimum arrangement if the car was going to be roomy and versatile. Against this, Volkswagen deduced its cars would soon be at a disadvantage, and in May 1968 chief executive Kurt Lotz ordered a major change of emphasis.

From now on, all efforts would be poured into front-engined, front-wheel drive automobiles with, crucially, water-cooled, in-line engines.

Did You Know?

In 1964, a young man took just 38 minutes to cross the Strait of Messina in his seagoing VW 1200, beating the regular ferry by 2 minutes. Another waterproofed example was piloted across the Irish Sea in 7½ hours, while Malcolm Buchanan also attempted a route from the Isle of Man to England; his car ran out of petrol 4 miles from the coast but was blown ashore by favourable winds.

◀ *Malcolm Buchanan on his perilous seven-and-a-half-hour voyage between the Isle of Man and the Cumbrian coast.*

A design classic but with a special claim to innovative fame: the 1971 Beetle was the first production car fitted with halogen-bulb headlights, made by Hella.

A great view of the Wolfsburg production line shortly before Beetle assembly ended there in 1974 to make way for the next Volkswagen phenomenon – the Golf.

The VW K70 came first, followed by the Passat, Scirocco and, in May 1974, the Golf.

The Beetle, of course, was still selling like hot cakes but the Golf's unprecedented newness in its mechanical layout under that sharp, Italian-styled (by Giorgetto Giugiaro) skin, with front-wheel drive and a transverse 'east–west' engine, showed the

future direction for Wolfsburg. The fact the Golf was an instant and huge sales success sealed the trusty Beetle's fate.

At 11.19 a.m. on 1 July 1974, the final Beetle rolled off its original Wolfsburg production line – the last of a rather epic 11,916,519. But German saloon manufacture would continue for another four years at Volkswagen's Emden factory, finally ending on 19 January 1978.

◀ The Volkswagen Golf of 1974 changed the company's direction forever, with a front-mounted, water-cooled engine driving the front wheels, and crisp new styling.

1974

➤ The Beetle turned into a spider for this eye-catching welding shop advert, somewhere in America 40 years ago.

◄ When Beetles crash, even the wrecks can be recycled, such as here where a Beetle's organs gave life to this wacky American motorised trike.

◄ No doubt the bride's mother was in tears when this Beetle-based swan wedding car turned up to make tacky an otherwise beautiful occasion. . . .

➤ Stickers on most cars of the 1970s tried to hide rust bubbles but, on the Beetle, they could simply turn it into a mobile scrapbook for your travelling mementoes.

◀ *The Karmann-built convertible, by the early 1970s, was one of the very few affordable four-seater soft-tops available.*

➤ *For those mourning the end of the open Beetle, Volkswagen had good news in 1980 – Karmann's Golf Cabriolet would be taking over, now equipped with a rollover bar.*

Did You Know?

German car magazine *Auto Motor und Sport* completed a mammoth road test of a Beetle 1303 in 1973 over two years and 70,000km. Despite receiving what the magazine called 'minimal care' it did not break down once and its paintwork still looked immaculate.

Even then, that wasn't quite the finish in the car's homeland because Karmann continued making the Convertible model until 10 January 1980; in 30 years, exactly 331,847 of those had found sun-worshipping owners. And even then, demand was such that brand new Beetles were still on sale, imported from Mexico, and remained so until 1985.

The ever-stylish convertible would be built by coachbuilder Karmann until 10 January 1980, making it the very last Beetle manufactured in Europe.

The work of keeping the old Beetle alive switched, from 1978, to Brazil. The engineers there had some novel ideas, including modifying the engine with twin copper-nickel-coated carburettors, a modified fuel pump and a tinplate fuel tank so that it could run on alcohol. Then, when Brazilian manufacture ceased in 1996, the technical development department switched to Mexico.

◄ *It's Mexico in May 1981 and another incredible production record is reached as the Beetle line just keeps on turning.*

89

Rather than put the lid of an old Beetle into the crusher, one enterprising farmer lashed it to his tractor, as a way to keep the dust out of his eyes.

Innumerable uses have been found for Beetles that are no longer roadworthy, such as this rustbucket turned into a turf roller for sports grounds in Switzerland.

It was here that the car would trickle past both the 20m mark in 1981 and the 21m record in 1992. Still, Mexican roads had been full of Beetles for years, and since 1971 the specially made 'Mexico Taxi' had been the staple cab in Mexico City, missing its front passenger seat so two paying customers could squeeze in behind the swarthy driver in what must rank as the most stifling taxi experience in the world.

➤ *The pretzel-shaped split-window of an early Volkswagen saloon meets the 20 millionth example in 1981 in a festival of automotive curvature.*

Did You Know?

Brasmotor was the Brazilian company that first assembled Volkswagen sedans in Brazil before VW took charge in São Paolo in 1953. The Germans then opened their own factory in São Bernardo do Campo in late 1956. Three years later, the 8,445 cars coming off the production line there in 1959 were made largely from locally produced components, and over 3.3m Beetle-type cars were then made in Brazil until 1986.

◄ This is the kind of publicity picture regularly issued by Volkswagen do Brasil as the company struggled to find much new to say about the cars it continued to churn out.

➤ It's usually the VW Kombi or camper van that gets surf dudes to the beach, although with a little ingenuity this 1303 convertible made a handy board-mobile.

◄ The very last of the original Beetles was built in 2003; note the Wolfsburg crest on the bonnet, the natty paint scheme and the whitewall tyres.

➤ *A 1980 Beetle rattling its way through the desolate beauty of rural Brazil, its driver assured there's no chance it'll overheat.*

Still, government subsidies put the vehicle within reach of impoverished cab drivers, and tens of thousands of them remain hard at work.

Mexican VW engineers oversaw the Beetle's final mechanical makeover when in 1993 the engine gained fuel-injection, hydraulic tappets, a Lambda probe oxygen sensor and a three-way catalytic converter for its exhaust system so it would meet both US-level Mexican and European Euro 3 emissions standards. Of course, it was common knowledge that the car's days were numbered, but by how much? In 2000, for instance, the Mexicans were still knocking out 170 of them every day – almost all going to taxi drivers, no doubt – and even three years later 53 cars a day were being built.

◄ *This 1985 edition of the Brazilian-made Beetle celebrates the car's 50th birthday with shiny paintwork and a special emblem.*

▼ *A consignment of newly-minted Beetles, along with a rogue Golf MkII, on their way across Mexico to expectant owners – taxi drivers, most likely – in the late 1980s.*

➤ *Porsche 911 Turbo tastes on a Beetle budget? Here's one German fan's faintly laughable attempt to bridge the gap.*

But the inevitable did, finally, happen on 30 July 2003, when the very last one was built in Puebla, Mexico.

It was part of a farewell 'Ultima edición' 1.6-litre series numbering 3,000 cars, all finished in either Aquarius blue or Harvest Moon beige with chrome trim, bumpers, hubcaps and door mirrors.

The final production total was 21,529,464 Beetles.

Once the Golf supplanted the Beetle as Volkswagen's mainstay in the 1970s, corporate favour naturally swung away from the old car. But, if anything, the Beetle's legend became even rosier – maybe as a reaction to the sameness most modern family cars exuded as manufacturers battled it out in rigidly defined market segments. The Beetle was massively popular in the classic car boom of the late 1970s and 1980s and then, as companies detected a groundswell of retro sentiment, Volkswagen designers naturally wondered how their brand could cash in on it.

Their ideas were presented to the public at the 1996 Geneva Motor Show with the Concept 1, a curvy little show car that evoked the friendly image of Dr Porsche's original. It was the dawn of the internet age, and early adopters mobbed Volkswagen's website with demands that the car be put into production. Whether this primitive on-line furore was actually whipped up by owners and admirers of the original we will probably never know, but VW certainly thought there was enough pent-up demand for a fun car like this that it gave the 'New Beetle' the go-ahead.

FACTS & DATA: VOLKSWAGEN NEW BEETLE

Announced: 1998
Engine capacity: 1983cc
Engine bore/stroke: 82.6/92.7mm
Engine power output: 115bhp @ 5200rpm
Fuel system: fuel-injection
Bodystyle: two-door, four-seater saloon
Wheelbase: 2520mm
Length: 4100mm
Width: 1730mm
Height: 1520mm
Top speed: 115mph
Acceleration, 0-62mph: 10.9sec
Fuel consumption, average: 32.5mpg approx
Price when new: £14,950 (in 2000)

The final style was penned by designer J. Mays in a studio in California. Its silhouette, rounded bonnet, curved roof, four bulbous wings, suggested running boards, large wheels and big, circular lights front and back were all pastiche copies of the original. The car had a notably light and airy interior, enlivened by witty touches like a built-in flower vase and a huge circular speedo, and was unthreatening in the extreme with its pastel tones, so hardly likely to chime with the Jeremy Clarkson mindset. Nor was it terribly practical, with a goldfish-bowl like feel inside yet not much leg- or headroom in the back.

In the nicest possible way, though, the New Beetle was a travesty of all that the original had stood for in terms of radical simplicity.

Did You Know?

There is just one component that is interchangeable between the original Type 1 Beetle and the Golf-based New Beetle. It's a rubber widget, part number 133,867,648, that used to stop the interior headlining rubbing on its frame and, in the New Beetle, is now used to secure the warning triangle in the boot. Symbolic or not, it's good to know.

◄ The Concept I of 1996 flew a kite for the idea of reinventing the Beetle, and drew a massive amount of attention from potential buyers.

◄ The New Beetle was quite a hit with the ladies, and some gentlemen. But underneath those fashionable clothes were the mechanical elements of the MkIV Golf in their entirety.

◄◄ This peach of a Beetle is from the 'Last Edition' series imported into the UK in 1978 and is lovingly treasured by Volkswagen UK to this day.

➤ *The New Beetle was launched in January 1998, and its retro design immediately split opinion between lovers and loathers.*

➤➤ *Often likened to a goldfish bowl, the New Beetle's interior included a flower vase.*

➤ That old pulling power: this traditionally-customised dragster Beetle still turns heads at the Santa Pod Raceway drag strip in Bedfordshire.

➤➤ With the popularity of the New Beetle, a convertible version was an inevitability. And don't they look good together, eh?

This one was front-engined, front-wheel-drive and water-cooled, and also a Golf-like hatchback with a folding rear seat in the back. It was a prime example of 'platform sharing' for, under the vaguely old-fashioned styling were the underpinnings of the VW Golf Mk IV, a rolling floorpan also shared with cars as diverse as the Skoda Octavia and the Audi TT.

The manufacture of the car began at the Mexican Puebla plant in December 1997 and it was a star at the Detroit Motor Show a month later. No doubt that deep US affection for the Beetle had helped bring it back, for the little car was as much about life in twentieth-century America as it was in Germany. Hence, the usual dry, cold, impartial criteria were cast aside to make the car North American Car of the Year.

On sale in mainland Europe from November 1998, UK demand was so strong Volkswagen decided to import 900 left-hand-drive versions into the country in April 1999 in advance of the first right-hand-drive versions arriving in January 2000. By 2002 there were four engine options, including 1.4-, 1.6- and 2.0-litre petrol, a 1.8 petrol turbo, and a 1.9 turbodiesel. All models came stuffed with the sort of goodies that the average German motorist of the early 1950s could only fantasise about, including six airbags, central locking, an immobiliser, anti-lock brakes, electronic stability control and electric windows.

Meanwhile, a Concept 1 convertible led, in January 2003, to a New Beetle Convertible that arrived in the UK that April. The electric roof took just 13 seconds to open or close, and automatic rollover protection was fitted as standard.

Being a car of the twenty-first century, of course, the New Beetle has to move with the times, with all the demand for frequent refreshes that entails.

◄ *The authentic stacked-hood look of the original Karmann was reproduced, although the car with an electrically-operated top as standard.*

◄ A delightful car for cruising along in on summer days, no New Beetle convertible was complete without its dahlia.

▼ With hood raised, the New Beetle looked pretty handsome, and was notably draught-proof inside.

➤ New Beetles both open and tin-topped were a popular choice in the UK, although sales began to slide when car buyers had had enough of 'retro'.

➤➤ In 2006 the New Beetle was given a visual makeover to update and smooth out the apparently 'timeless' design.

Hence, the 2006 cars were given a comprehensive facelift, with little styling tweaks everywhere even down to the lights and badges. It was, after all, in stiff competition with the New MINI and, shortly, the New Fiat 500 too, both of them modern-day interpretations of classic 'people's cars'. These are, moreover, fickle times, with New Beetles sales peaking in the UK in 2004 when 9,179 were sold but slumping to 2,193 in 2009.

Some cars are blokes' cars – in fact, most cars, being generally designed by men, are blokes' cars, even if women have the overwhelming final say on purchase decisions – and some cars are strictly girls' cars. The New Beetle, by its whole demeanour and ambience, was in the latter camp. Car magazines (generally written by blokes) have no qualms in saying so, such as America's *Car and Driver*: 'Throughout its 73-year history, the VW Beetle has embodied VW's "people's car" philosophy. . . . It was only during the 12-year term of the New Beetle that those people became, by and large, female. In its peak year, the New Beetle sold more than 80,000 copies in the US, roughly 75 per cent of them to women, based on our observation. (The other 25 per cent going to very effeminate, very confident, or completely oblivious men).'

So when it came to replacing the New Beetle, Volkswagen listened to its macho critics and decided that a shot of testosterone was urgently required to get the car talked about in pubs, bars, football stadia and male-orientated internet forums across the world. In 2011, the new car – now no longer the New Beetle, just plain Beetle – was unveiled. It looked meaner, more aggressive and more purposeful.

As *Car and Driver* grunted with approval, the car was reshaped 'so it will appeal to more than just people who can get away with wearing skirts in public (Scots excluded). Gone is the syrupy-cute, large-bubble-eating-a-smaller-bubble appearance, replaced by a design with a flatter, lower roof, a flatter, longer hood, and tauter sheet metal that looks like someone popped a pressure-relief valve and bled off a couple of dozen psi.'

➤ *Love for Beetles and the Herbie films is strong and lasting, as this parade of aficionados and their cars in Berlin in 2006 showed.*

▲ When Volkswagen's early thoughts turned to a replacement for the New Beetle, a rather more aggressive direction was decided upon.

In fact, the roofline was only half an inch lower but the 2.3in wider and 6in longer body, along with clever restyling, made all the difference.

As before, the car is front-engined and driven, sharing its hardware with the contemporary Volkswagen Jetta, and the wide range of engines (which starts at 1.2 and rises to 2.0 litres), includes a choice of turbodiesels, and extends to a 2.5-litre five-cylinder unit for the US market. A six-speed manual gearbox or dual-clutch automatic is available optionally with all of them.

Inside, much improved luggage capacity is helped by a 50:50 split folding rear seat.

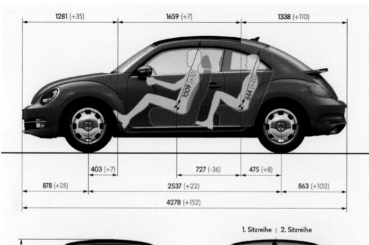

1281 (+35)   1659 (+7)   1338 (+110)

1009 (+10)   844 (+60)

403 (+7)   727 (-36)   475 (+8)

878 (+28)   2537 (+22)   863 (+102)

4278 (+152)

1. Sitzreihe | 2. Sitzreihe

1486 (-12)

1578 (+63)   345 (+12)   270 (-30)

1808 (+84)   1404 (+64)   1245 (-23)

2021 (+36)   1544 (+49)

Did You Know?

Volkswagen created a very special New Beetle in the limited edition RSI (only 250 made from 2001–3). The four-wheel-drive performance model boasted a 224bhp 3.2-litre 24-valve VR6 engine, a Remus twin-tailpipe exhaust system, race-tuned suspension, widened wheelarches, a prominent rear aerofoil and special OZ alloy wheels. The Recaro racing seats were trimmed in lurid orange leather. A couple of the left-hand-drive cars came to the UK, at £50,000 each.

◄ *These graphics show how company bosses wanted to make sure that a 21st century Beetle would be a capacious four-seater.*

◄◄ Some of
Volkswagen's Mexican
workforce with the first
Beetles off the line in
autumn 2011.

◄ From this angle, the
all-new car perhaps looks
most like the original
Beetle in overall shape.

◄◄ *Vivid leather seats and bright metal accents add some verve to a sporty and purposeful interior environment.*

◄ *Enormous doors make getting into the back of the Beetle a cinch, in stark comparison to the contortions required in previous cars.*

◀◀ *A significant victim of Volkswagen's drive to make the latest Beetle more macho were the circular rear lights, replaced by sleek, wraparound clusters.*

◀ *As much as the 2011 Beetle has been made more conventional, it is still one of the most distinctive new cars on the road today.*

◄◄ *Drive a Volkswagen Beetle (or camper van) and relaxed days out are a must; at festivals and sports events as much as at car shows, fellow enthusiasts will always want to discuss your car's finer points.*

◄ *There's always something to do with an old Volkswagen – such as, turn it into a greenhouse-cum-plant pot to give your seeds and cuttings a good start in life.*

126

Needless to say, the flower vase is no longer fitted, but a neat tribute to the past are the two gloveboxes, recalling the two 'Beetle bins' of the original 1940s cars.

The process to normalise the Beetle is pretty much done. Apart from its rounded profile, the current car is about as conformist as it could be. Distinctive, yes, but its character is a processed nod to a world-beating original that went its own way and made it purely on its right place/right time merits. No doubt, in the car world we won't see the radical likes of Dr Porsche's people's car ever again. Considering some of the dodgy political ethos surrounding its birth, some might say that's a good thing. Meanwhile, millions of air-cooled, rear-engined, oh-so-cool, Type 1 Beetle survivors just keep on going.

◀ *Very different in execution but united in spirit, this study contrasts old and new convertibles.*

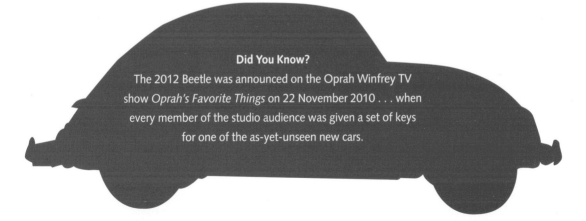

Did You Know?
The 2012 Beetle was announced on the Oprah Winfrey TV show *Oprah's Favorite Things* on 22 November 2010 . . . when every member of the studio audience was given a set of keys for one of the as-yet-unseen new cars.

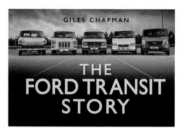

■ ISBN 978 07524 6281 3

■ ISBN 978 07524 6282 0

■ ISBN 978 07524 6283 7

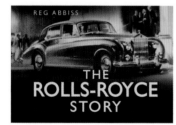

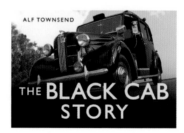

■ ISBN 978 07524 6614 9

■ ISBN 978 07509 4853 1

■ ISBN 978 07524 5084 1